WILD WORK

Who Swings the Wrecking Ball?

WORKING ON A CONSTRUCTION SITE

Mary Meinking

Raintree

Chicago, Illinois

www.heinemannraintree.com
Visit our website to find out
more information about
Heinemann-Raintree books.

To order:

☎ Phone 888-454-2279

▭ Visit www.heinemannraintree.com
to browse our catalog and order online.

Edited by David Andrews, Nancy Dickmann, and Rebecca
Rissman
Designed by Victoria Allen
Picture research by Liz Alexander
Leveled by Marla Conn, with Read-Ability.
Originated by Dot Gradations Ltd
Printed and bound in China by Leo Paper Products Ltd

15 14 13 12 11 10
10 9 8 7 6 5 4 3 2 1

Library of Congress Cataloging-in-Publication Data
Meinking, Mary.
  Who swings the wrecking ball? : working on a construction
site / Mary Meinking.
      p. cm.—(Wild work)
  Includes bibliographical references and index.
  ISBN 978-1-4109-3854-1 (hc)—ISBN 978-1-4109-3863-3
(pb) 1. Construction workers—Juvenile literature.
2. Building—Equipment and supplies—Juvenile literature.
I. Title. II. Title: Working on a construction site.
  TH149.C43 2011
  690—dc22   2009050295

Acknowledgements
The author and publisher are grateful to the following for
permission to reproduce copyright material:

Alamy pp. **15** (© Dan Leeth), **17** (© [apply pictures]), **21**
 (© Ken Welsh); Corbis pp. **4** (© Michael Reynolds/epa), **7**
(© Andy Kingsbury), **24** (© Lance Nelson/Stock Photos), **25**
(© Jack Hollingsworth), **27** (© Don Mason); Getty Images
pp. **20** (Joel Rogers/Stone), **22** (Lester Lefkowitz/Stone);
Masterfile Corporation p. **9** (Boden/Ledingham); Photolibrary
pp. **12** (White), **13** (John Lund/Drew Kelly/Blend Images),
14 (Ralph Kerpa/imagebroker.net), **16** (Gary Moon/age
footstock), **23** (Steve Dunwell/Index Stock Imagery),
26 (Chris Windsor/White), **28** (Granger Wootz/Blend Images);
Shutterstock pp. **5** (© Anton Gvozdikov), **6** (© djgis), **8**
(© 4634093993), **10** (© Doug Stevens), **11** (© Doug Stevens),
18 (© Faraways), **19** (© Khafizov Ivan Harisovich), **29**
(© Feraru Nicolae).

Background design features reproduced with permission
of Shutterstock (©Xtremer).

Cover photograph reproduced with permission of Corbis
(©Construction Photography).

We would like to thank Roshan Mehdizadeh for her invaluable
help in the preparation of this book.

Every effort has been made to contact copyright holders of
any material reproduced in this book. Any omissions will
be rectified in subsequent printings if notice is given to
the publisher.

Disclaimer
All the Internet addresses (URLs) given in this book were valid
at the time of going to press. However, due to the dynamic
nature of the Internet, some addresses may have changed, or
sites may have changed or ceased to exist since publication.
While the author and publisher regret any inconvenience this
may cause readers, no responsibility for any such changes can
be accepted by either the author or the publisher.

Some words are shown in bold, **like this.** You can find
out what they mean by looking in the glossary.

Contents

From the Ground Up 4

Big Bang! 6

Get to Work! 12

Monster Machines. 14

Skeleton Walkers 20

Liquid Stone 22

Knock on Wood 24

Bright Idea 26

Could You Work on a Construction Site? . 28

Glossary 30

Find Out More 31

Index 32

From the Ground Up

Grab your hardhat for a look at construction sites. Construction is dangerous work. Sparks fly, wheels crush, and sometimes things explode!

Construction workers build everything from homes to schools to offices. But let's see how the tallest buildings, **skyscrapers,** are made!

Big Bang!

Demolition (say *dem-UH-lish-un*) experts get paid to smash things! They are in charge of safely destroying buildings. Some buildings aren't safe or are too old. They need to be knocked down to make room for new ones.

jackhammer

There are many ways to destroy buildings. Small buildings are broken apart with noisy **jackhammers**.

Some large buildings are torn down with an **excavator** (say *ek-ska-VAY-tor*). Workers use the excavator's claw-like arm to rip apart walls and floors.

excavator

Sometimes workers use a wrecking ball to smash old buildings. The heavy ball swings from a tall **crane**. It crashes into the building again and again until it tumbles down.

wrecking ball

The quickest way to get rid of a tall building is to blow it up! **Demolition** experts place **explosives** in a building. When everyone's far away, a signal sets them off. Kaboom!

DID YOU KNOW?

First the bottom floors of a building blow up. Then the top floors crash down, like a stack of pancakes! Once the dust settles, all that's left is a pile of **rubble**.

Get to Work!

The boss on a construction site is the **superintendent**. The superintendent says which workers, machines, and supplies are needed each day.

blueprints

Superintendents read the **blueprints** to keep workers' jobs in order. They check that everyone's work is done right and on time.

Monster Machines

The land must be cleared to make room for a new building. That's the backhoe operator's job. These big machines roar into action!

backhoe

Operators push foot pedals or buttons to make their machines move. A joystick controls the machines actions.

Bulldozers have a curved blade on the front. They shove heavy things and smooth the ground. Bulldozers run on a track so they won't get stuck.

track

Once the land is cleared, **excavators** roll in. The huge bucket digs basements and makes holes for **foundations**. **Skyscrapers** need strong foundations so they won't fall over.

The bed, or back, of a dump truck is filled with dirt and rocks. The drivers take the load to the dump site. The front of the bed is lifted. Everything crashes out the back.

bed

DID YOU KNOW?

A regular dump truck can carry enough sand to fill 34 sandboxes. But monster dump trucks could fill 1,150 sandboxes!

Skeleton Walkers

Iron workers make the inside frames of **skyscrapers**. Sparks fly when they **weld** together the steel "skeletons" of the buildings.

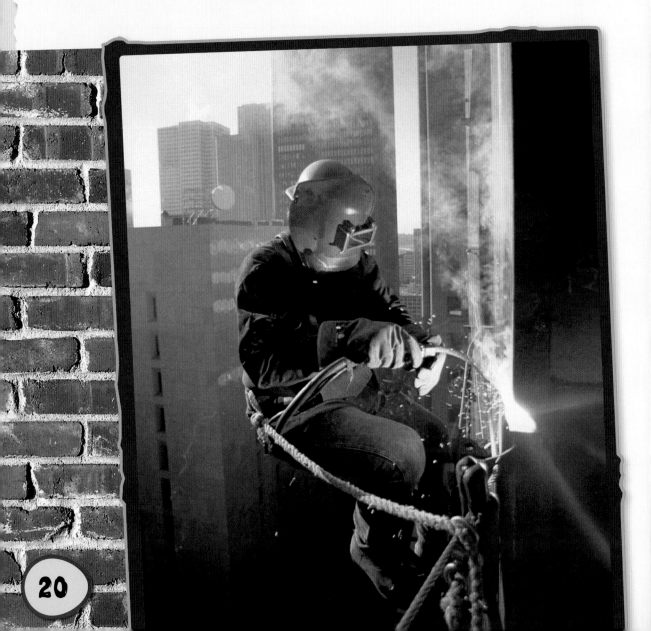

safety net

Iron workers have dangerous jobs. They work on beams high in the air. But they wear safety belts to catch them if they fall. Nets catch materials that may accidentally drop.

Liquid Stone

Concrete is used for the building's **foundation** and walls. Workers make molds to hold the concrete. Trucks bring soft concrete to the site.

concrete

Workers use pumps to pour the mushy concrete into the molds. Then they smooth it out with long, flat rakes. It dries as hard as a rock.

Knock on Wood

Carpenters don't just use hammers and nails. They use power tools such as electric drills, saws, and sanders. Sawdust flies when they're at work!

saw

Some of these tools can be dangerous. Never use them without an adult to help you.

nail gun

Most carpenters use nail guns. The nail gun uses air to shoot nails into the wood.

Bright Idea

Electricians hook up electricity in new buildings. Electricity powers heating, cooling, lights, outlets, phones, computers, and smoke alarms.

Like many workers at a construction site, electricians wear a special belt to keep all their tools handy.

Could You Work on a Construction Site?

Construction workers need to be able to follow directions. They should be good at working with their hands. Everyone must work as a team.

DID YOU KNOW?

The tallest **skyscraper** is the Burj Khalifa. It is more than ½ mile (almost 1 km) tall! It took more than 7,500 construction workers to build it.

Glossary

blueprint drawn plan showing how a building needs to be made

bulldozer machine used to push heavy things

carpenter worker who makes or repairs wooden things

concrete soft building material that dries hard

crane machine used to lift and carry heavy things

demolition destroying something on purpose

electrician person who sets up electricity in a building

excavator a machine that digs or carries materials

explosive material used to break things apart with force

foundation underground part of a building that keeps it strong

jackhammer a large drill used to break things up

joystick a lever that controls a machine

rubble pieces of things that have been broken apart

superintendent person in charge of workers on a construction site

skyscraper a very tall building

weld using heat to melt together metal pieces

Find Out More

Books to Read

Alinas, Marv. *Bulldozers.* (*Machines at Work series*). Mankato, MN: The Child's World, 2008.

Macken, JoAnn Early. *Building a Skyscraper.* Mankato, MN: Capstone Press, 2008.

Web Sites to Visit

http://www.pbs.org/wgbh/buildingbig/
Explore skyscrapers and what it takes to build them. This site follows the "Building Big" books and TV series.

http://www.bobthebuilder.com/usa/games.asp
Bob the Builder activities, games, projects, and videos about construction.

http://www.kenkenkikki.jp/special/e_index.html
Learn about construction equipment, with games, videos, and a coloring contest. This site even lets you e-mail construction equipment greeting cards.

Index

backhoes 14–15
basements 17
blades 16
blueprints 13
buckets 17
bulldozers 16
Burj Khalifa skyscraper 29

carpenters 24–25
concrete 22–23
cranes 9

danger 4, 21, 25
demolition 6–10, 11
demolition experts 6, 10
dump trucks 18, 19

electricians 26
electricity 24, 26
excavators 8, 17
explosives 10, 11

foundations 17, 22
frames 20

iron workers 20–21

jackhammers 7
joysticks 15

molds 22, 23

nail guns 25

power tools 24, 25

safety 6, 21
skyscrapers 17, 20, 29
superintendents 12–13

teamwork 28
tracks 16
trucks 18, 19, 22

walls 8, 22
welding 20
wrecking balls 9